hibernation, a hush

poems by

Grace Covill-Grennan

Finishing Line Press
Georgetown, Kentucky

hibernation, a hush

Copyright © 2021 by Grace Covill-Grennan
ISBN 978-1-64662-499-7 First Edition
All rights reserved under International and Pan-American Copyright Conventions. No part of this book may be reproduced in any manner whatsoever without written permission from the publisher, except in the case of brief quotations embodied in critical articles and reviews.

ACKNOWLEDGMENTS

I'd like to acknowledge the wonderful publications in which the following poems were first published:

"little girl blue"and "should we talk about it?" in *Heirlock Magazine*
"the knife" in *Little Stone Journal*
"virga" in *Timshel Magazine*
"February" and "hibernation, a hush" under the title "head trip" in *Genre: Urban Arts*
"light pollution;" "so long" under the title "so long, Eliot;" and "utterance" in *Wild Roof Journal*
"postcard home" in *Permafrost Magazine*
"worn in" in *Timberline Review*
"drinking with the Powell hand crew" in *Rockford Review*
"crownless" in *Rockvale Review*

I extend my particular appreciation to those who helped read and offer feedback on these poems: Amy Covill, Mitch Neuber, Rosie Sokolov, and Joe Rupprecht.

Publisher: Leah Huete de Maines
Editor: Christen Kincaid
Cover Art: Grace Covill-Grennan
Author Photo: Thiện Nguyễn Minh, http://roefoto.art/
Cover Design: Elizabeth Maines McCleavy

Order online: www.finishinglinepress.com
also available on amazon.com

Author inquiries and mail orders:
Finishing Line Press
PO Box 1626
Georgetown, Kentucky 40324
USA

Table of Contents

queen milkweed 1

little girl blue 3

Ophelia redux 4

the knife 6

virga 7

February 8

light pollution 9

should we talk about it? 10

not back together 11

so long 13

hibernation, a hush 14

utterance 15

postcard home 16

drinking with the Powell hand crew 17

worn in 19

our quarters 21

crownless 23

brine 24

To my friends and family

queen milkweed

go ahead, pick it apart at the seams
lean into the wheeze & drag of the saw
just be soft, swooping & available as milkweed
crowned & spanning as a hewn beam
god knows I can't, see, it's in my jaw
it's in the scarred fingers I bury as dead seeds

eyes stare into lids like dead seeds
any way you cut it there has to be a seam
remembering your talk clenches my jaw
I'd better cut you out but there's no such saw
instead I'll narrow, reduce to a balancing beam
til all I'm stuffed with scatters, numb as milkweed

if I had a baby I'd sew it a quilt batted with milkweed
I do have hot shame, a clutch of dead seeds
& amnesiac light falling down in a beam
the quilt, though, would have finely pressed seams
broken dishes, flying geese, crossroads of arkansas
it would swaddle my darling from toes up to jaw

daybreak runs a finger along my jaw
night's rotting pod fallen open as milkweed
today I'll dress, eat, oil my saw
grind a coarse meal from the meat of dead seeds
crush the lice that make their lives in my seams
hang harmless hooks from a notched, sagging beam

no I can't reveal the spell that made your ghost beam
down & land a playful punch on my jaw
for my craft isn't what it sometimes seems
no tail of rat or down of milkweed
no cursed spinning wheels or worshipping dead seeds
I just waste time writing down what I saw

but turns out, what I see everyone already saw
& they all went off drunk to swing from a beam
while I bent my back hoeing beds for dead seeds
in a hot field, in the west, sweat running off my jaw
mallow, purslane, chicory, milkweed
I'll tuck their currencies into my mattress seam

I've had it, see, with floating in beams, dropping my jaw,
& these decadent sawyers who namedrop milkweed
fruitlessly panning for dead seeds in a spent ruby seam

little girl blue

morning filled with dew
little girl blue
buttons up a wool skirt
chews the food, sips
the glass of yellow juice
it's time to walk to school
walk through blue lockers
through bells & rules
into thighs bruised blue
into blue & white pills
blue girl left class
to skip smooth rocks across
the Susquehanna, smoke reds
lick blue powder from
wild sloe fruit
wander through
sallow lamplight pools
nighttime isn't cruel
it's cooler, a loose mood
small stars, umber sky
wan, low moon
& time an endless spool
unwinding slowly for you
irresolute girl comes home
to a room of tv blue,
mother's long look, unamused
little girl blue
you'll be what you choose

Ophelia redux

*an arrangement of verses
from Shakespeare's Hamlet,
with a few modifications*

they say the owl was a baker's daughter
lord, we know what we are
but know not what we may be

let's have no words of this
but when they ask you what it means
say you this: tomorrow
is saint valentine's day
& I a maid at your window
to be your valentine
a reckless libertine
the primrose path of dalliance
to tread
though 'tis
but brief

words of so sweet breath composed
bended their light on me
& I have remembrances
of yours
that I have longed long
to re-deliver
I pray you
now receive them
their perfume lost
take these again

but we must be patient
'tis brief

there's pansies
for thoughts
there's fennel for you
& columbines
here's rue for you
& some is mine

I cannot choose but to weep
tears seven times salt
do you doubt that?
I, of ladies most deject
& wretched
suck'd the honey—
I was the more deceived

heavenly powers
larded with sweet flowers
come, my coach
good night ladies
good night sweet ladies
good night, good night

the knife
      after Elizabeth Bishop

this is the knife
the right hand used
to cut the left

this is the man
who gave me the knife
that slipped from the right hand
to cut the left

this is the hate
I grew for the man
who gave me the knife
the right hand used
to cut the left

this is the scar
grown over the hate
I nursed for the man
who gave me the knife
my right hand used
to cut my left

this is your touch
numb over the scar
left by the hate
that saved me from the man
who gave me the knife
I took in my right hand
to cut my left

virga

under the dripping blue
tarp, ironically short on water
we cooked cous cous
in PBR, ate unworried
pine boughs flailed below
blameless stars

I'm remembering myself
& us, as we were
how I'd hoped to draw
the world around my throat
like a velvet cloak

February

olde english shards
dumpster slam
smoky breath under streetlights
invisible stars
glittering dog shit

*I wouldn't want to watch me
destroy myself either*

these memories have me
shaking my head involuntarily
fucking
what the fuck ever

you didn't used to be like this

well
getting angry about it
won't help anything

numb fingers
nobody's fault
cold air invades
my chest, breaks it
into two lungs
& a pinch of dust

light pollution

i.

clouds spoon feed a diminished moon
to the city's sick, slackened maw
jagged orange horizon devouring
the day in an exhaust-laced swoon

white lilac flowers: little
paper trumpets littered
in a quiet, mossy gutter
on my walk home through
streetlight spillover

ii.

lying in bed listening to the block
still lit up behind my pillowcase curtain
a nocturnal drone
in the park across the street
compression brakes on the 26

iii.

just before sleep I'm visited
by the mosquito hawk's memory
I found it dead on my pillow
after work today
its filament legs chaotically arrayed
as I lifted it to my open window
it seemed to weigh
absolutely nothing

should we talk about it?

alone at the pond
cold beer, new lure
warm, wide raindrops
purple clouds fume
above green hills

a trout's white flash amid murk
tugs & disappears; its power,
freedom, wholeness
preserved

berries at the bottom of my tin pail
a small drumroll as I walk
I plucked a perfect huckleberry
& it fell from my fingers
to a hidden place below

things will be better
if you just
let me go

not back together

some people really don't know when to quit
this place proctors test after test of my mettle
ballsy mice run their mouths about how the grits
turned out, my sleepy feet doze off at the pedals
& I'm still out here pruning emotions like hazardous limbs
mold blooming through carefully whitewashed pine trim

while fit as a fiddle, faulty as a fuse, & trimmed
as a partridge you lurk under the bridge, peddle
remedies with ramifications & evenings you limb
me down to a pole, chainsaw choked up with grit
your heart isn't in it but you're too deep to quit
so I bite down on my lip til I taste red metal

but shit, least I'm learning, like don't fucking meddle
with insomniac optimists who offer you a trim
or that dying's the only for-sure way of quitting
saw you out at the bar last month ripping petal
after petal off some fresh flower, just gritting
those teeth, clawing your way back from out on a limb

enough reminiscing, though, I'm fine, still got one good limb
to hold onto through nights forged of dull metal
yeah yeah you strung me out, stripped off my grit
but you're in a worse way, got stuck hanging trim
& tinsel from one tough tannenbaum, limp as a petal,
saddled with salaried habits you can't afford to quit

as for me? seems like what I do best is quit
hang my hat each night on some novel limb
I just go day to day, hand to mouth, crank the pedals
fashion a shelter from torn tarps & war medals
hitch up too-small britches, gather what others trim
off, serve it hot in the morning with collards & grits

early, long before, and even after the grits
this intractable moaning of pipes never quits
I go about my morning, touching up window trim
expressing myself through a puppet's dead limbs
I don't stick my beak in, pry, snoop, or meddle
you might say I'm self-contained as a petal

what with dim futures to limn, fresh theories to peddle
not to mention the grit, the molds, the chisel, the metal
I'll quit this heart another year & trim whatever's not too dear

so long

I'm changing changing
changing changing
bitter turn peeling birch
pregnant silence re-arranging
change to a bitch sway & lurch
micro violence went to church
was unmade the host upbraided
lost my clothes was re-created
highly tithed bared incisor
bummed a smoke from my baptizer
divination rod to find you
shamefaced in a shadowed pew
was it you? was that
you?

****

the truth
is you will never
change, is you are
beautiful &
very far away
& the world forever
world forever hunter
green & I a green
leaf turning over, changing, new

hibernation, a hush

the October before I turn 22
I'm trudging up a snowy slope
with two friends and a broken heart
hallucinating that there are
shining, charged rows
of dots, lines, & arrows
inhabiting, animating the dark trees
midnight observes without comment
our crooked tracks & deranged laughter

in a wide clearing we stop & watch
with wordless terror as a massive husky
runs silently out of the woods toward us
the dog slows, sniffs with mild interest
at my dangling scarf then runs on into the far forest
on a personal errand, not to be delayed
my mouth is open as I watch it run away

yeah there was that spooky moonlight
people love to bring up, green needles,
we exchanging breath with sleepy trees,
hibernation, a hush, then hot self-consciousness

it's all this trying to articulate things that throws me
the crude pliers of language effing up the ineffable

like shouting how I love the lightness of snow
into a soon-to-be avalanche's poised echo

utterance

fuzzy snore of needle left
on spooled out record
hypnosis suture dim abstraction
become a voice
become a voice

hair leaking from behind my love's ear
languid gesture wild liquid
become a voice
become a voice

shudder soft apology
shoulder blades plough under
sleep-soft pilled cables
protrude like stubbed out
wings—blackbird
beckon, speak a word

****

through the foam & trailing kelp
of our days the refrigerator
opens & closes omissions
rattle in the oval eaves
mute palms scoop salt & almonds
into the void between my lips
cave in on neonate notions
& no ghosts emerge from this
icy, thousand pound ocean

I wish I could have shown you
white cranes with black wingtips
unison lazy susan murmuration
revolving feathers flashed
bright & woven as voices

postcard home

writing this
in a pull-off
on the outskirts
of Ukiah
dark pines
white sky
my phone
is useless
my pack soft
fragrant & loose

dry socks, soap
bad coffee &
a $6 shower
Patsy Cline playing
in the general store
does a body good

in a dream
I was cutting
off locks
of my
hair
to fall
as sable
blazes
beside
the narrow
trail
missing you

drinking with the Powell hand crew

on the porch outside the Lochsa Lodge's bar
my drinking companions' faces are blacked out by the bright row of
    windows behind them.
the same windows which illuminate & expose my face to them. these
    young men.
fresh off shift, they drink their beer straight from pitchers.
one of them asks me a question, then resumes talking before I can
    form a sentence.
keep up! one has got to keep pace in this world.
they pass around a tin of snuff tobacco, take doses with the tip of a
    knife & snort them.
one of them keeps calling me Mitch's wife.
who the hell are these people? how did I wind up here?
inside, a weathered specimen in wranglers sits at the bar,
an open carry pistol on his belt, watching basketball.
what a country.
as I drink I become increasingly loud & boorish. try passionately to
    talk
about labor militancy & the mine wars, but grow confused.
who knows what they think of me?
the one I like has a tattoo of a hissing black cat's face on the back of his
    right hand
& a forked tongue that his cousin back in North Carolina slit for him:
    felt like a long paper cut
what response to that can I be expected to produce?

later on, in bed, it's raining, it's pouring
my old man is snoring
this distinct spinning sensation forebodes
an unpleasant morning to come
& I'd just like to point out
that I've been provided with precious
little assistance in making sense of all this
yes yes I'm in good company but
at the bitter end, at the gnawed cob of it
we're each thrown back on our own meager resources

not to complain, just as context I guess

or something
maybe an apology

worn in

living for the weekend, spend-thrift thrills, handy young hammer
for hire said I need a raise & the boss said then go climb
a ladder; you can tell so much by a person's grammar
for example me putting shoes on before pants, unable to refrain
so eager, so excited to maybe dissolve into the sublime this time
to just spin & spin & fall down onto a calico prairie's infinite plane

my resume states I am a hard worker, though rather plain
it's ok, I mostly use it to plug holes my hammer
made; fly got away but won't be so lucky next time
yes the aluminum kind's the only ladder I'm equipped to climb
it's all I can do to look busy & come in strong on the refrain,
from the diaphragm, feeling the words, relishing the grammar

measure once, cut it right the first time god damn it: the grammar
of apprenticeship, back & forth rasp of the block plane
cry about it, laugh about it, snooze the alarm, same refrain
close my eyes at night & see waffle prints on wood my hammer
leaves, working for it, driving all over Portland, crawling, climbing
it's all the same slipping by of finite, unceremonious time

laughing to myself it all hits me in the truck after quitting time
each day may say something different but they use the same grammar
wears a body out, these stairs you just descend as soon as you climb
in bed listening to the sighs of the train, let me make this plain:
I do feel a certain swarming buzz making its nest in my hammering
chest, a terrestrian aptness, an ease & familiarity with the refrain

but if once I indulge a thirsty urge, henceforth I find it hard to refrain
to avoid bad thoughts, turns of mind, I keep busy in the meantime
safely between the bumpers of routine: day's end, roll cords, hammers
roost in their loops, tuck tarps, all things have an order, a grammar
there's a shimming & sanding that could bring it all into plane
just arrive at 7, with a degree of masochism & a willingness to climb

you'd think after all the falls I would lose this itching desire to climb
I try staying low but always rise with the rousing refrain
in a dream I walked out forever into the rabbit-strewn plain
then woke up to your irish goodbye, thinking how we can't know the
    time
we're given, all we can do is sleep in, haul lumber, obey the week's
    grammar
drink & take turns hitting nails into a stump with a hammer

these days I feel fine whatever my allotment, I don't waste time to
    complain
finding it better to refrain from correcting the world's grammar
I just stay in my lane as the speedometer climbs & chilly pistons
    hammer

our quarters

i.
windowsill dough risen
felt slipper robin's nest
snowdrop whisk laundry list
fawn fence patchwork kiss
long yawn bleeding heart
furrow crisp needlework
salsify pasture cleanse
lamb wound dye birth
reckon spoon basket hens
embroider alphabet root broth
thaw fever scour knead
scatter flour lesson froth
skim cream deft bead
duckling paddle sharp spade
postcard tincture fleecy maid

ii.
leather glove loamy trowel
moths worship yellow light
porch murmurs ashtray euchre
wending trail ninebark bite
stump throne smoky plaid
sunlight frayed bedspread quilt
tilt up timber trouble's braids
stifling attic hammock cloud
dock rifle ripple buckhorn
sawdust oar fishhook knot
creaky fir oat straw burlap
rusted pickup dusty road
kitchen bustle cousins nap
cellar backyard blessed hose
bumble clothesline apron ties
pocketknife porch rail pies
stout bales lemon balm
trout scales on a calloused palm

iii.
threadbare veil threshold fog
ribbon bow red red red
weave hem whorl fallow
haul farewell helmless plough
smolder leaves clove mull
twixt rough hewn hollow
halves moon haunt this heart
halt holding unlatched hasp
scythe heave damp behold
hasty shadow hammer heft
hallowed kindling chalice
heathen garland hearth
harrow gather quicken
trim the wicks & hail
hail all hail
our muddy boot strings

iv.
mugwort holly sweeping broom
stocking ember greeny bough
woolen long johns firewood
glitter brick drafty wink
jack frost recipe
goose down nightcap twine
wither fuming candle wicks
old dog silver bells
steam boilo antler sheds
twilight steadfast tannenbaum
glow sweet kindred song:
ah poor bird take thy flight
high above the shadows
of this dark night

crownless

I'll sing with my bare soles
flat to the spare wooden floor
old words will show their shapes
to my warm, tender mouth

the minute motes of untended
places rise in mute praise
my cool dark hair floats loose
ghostly insubordinate strands

blessed notes exult scored hands
salute all budless boughs
rainy ruts in muddy roads
hail to witches waifs & widows

hail to mothers' midnight vigils
hummed hymns, bedside carols
singing smiths my memory light, light
light & lilting as the crownless

brine

whilst my strong limbs yet the shroud evade, voice raised
I belong in the lewd loudness of the crew's rowdy singing
by night rolled-up sleeves & sound houses my sleep-talk praises
by day I chop blocks & finger carefree confetti for flinging
timelessness, temptation, light-hearted leaving
I spin within arms 'til I can't tell laughing from heaving

sway & reel down the deck, the sea pitching & heaving
after all night taking my fill of sins, deep-fried rays
& fists pounding my bare chest, I'm leaving
stepping right off a plank while lustily singing
of strong drink, keel hauling, & fishing pole flinging
but first, just before, I stiffly kneel down & pray

for protection from sharks who would make me their prey
just when I meant to pronounce the amen, heaving
from seasickness overtook me instead, & flinging
myself back onto the boards my dehydrated eyes skyward I raise
& thus prone am transported by heavenly singing
back to you, your homespun beauty unleaving

your scarf & raw knuckles as robins were leaving
your seltzer, long johns, warm ears in song I praise
& like Briar Rose am revived by the mere act of singing
my sleek throat, clotted lungs, & hands hard with heaving
the halyard & cranking at pegs the deep anchor to raise
all return commanding I dispatch with foam flinging

to exult in the thatch of your homemade haircut, flinging
arms around your body, kick off clogs cobbled for leaving
& hammer in hand a humble haunt for our home raise
I'll sit across from your face, ecstatically praise
the five fiber casserole I can eat without heaving,
& listen enraptured to your soft bathroom singing

bracingly brought back to life by bright singing,
bruised knees, a hangover, & joyful rice flinging
your big hands held my hair through a morning of heaving
then laid me on my back to gaze at the trees' green leaving
you whispered even the pope just moves his lips when he prays
& we slept there together under the sun's heavy rays

these ragged remains of singing pulled from sea air are soon leaving
but the last choppy throes & heaves without sadness I praise
my arms engaged in worthy flinging & four strong walls for you I raised

Grace Covill-Grennan lives in Enterprise, OR. She has worked variously as a school counselor, carpenter, farmer, youth shelter counselor, cook, nanny, and house cleaner. Her poetry has appeared in *Thin Air Magazine, Little Stone Journal, Permafrost Magazine, Rockford Review,* and others. She is the author of the mixed-genre book *Blockhead* (Another New Calligraphy Press, 2019), and was a writer in residence at Art Farm Nebraska in 2019.

www.ingramcontent.com/pod-product-compliance
Lightning Source LLC
LaVergne TN
LVHW041516070426
835507LV00012B/1607